ACTION EVENTS

MUD

RACING

ACTION EVENTS

MUD RACING

BY JEFF SAVAGE

CRESTWOOD HOUSE
Parsippany, New Jersey

Photo Credits
(all photos) United States Hot Rod Association.
Cover and book design by Liz Kril

Published by Crestwood House,
A Division of Simon and Schuster,
299 Jefferson Road, Parsippany, NJ 07054

First Edition
Printed in the United States of America
10 9 8 7 6 5 4 3 2 1

Library of Congress Cataloging-in-Publication Data
Savage, Jeff, 1961–
      Mud racing / by Jeff Savage. — 1st ed.
                  p. cm.—(Action events)
      Includes index.

      Summary: Provides an introduction to mud racing. Discusses the object, rules, and dangers of the motorsport as well as famous drivers, events, and vehicles.

      ISBN 0-89686-888-5 (lib. bdg.)—ISBN 0-382-39297-3 (pbk.)

      1. Mud racing—Juvenile literature. [1. Mud racing. 2. Automobile racing.] I. Title. II. Series:
Savage, Jeff, 1961–   Action events.
GV1029.9.M83S28 1997
796.7—dc2   95-32757

CAMEL
MUD & MONSTER
SERIES
CAMEL
MUD & MONSTER
SERIES
CAMEL
MUD & MONSTER
SERIES

CONTENTS

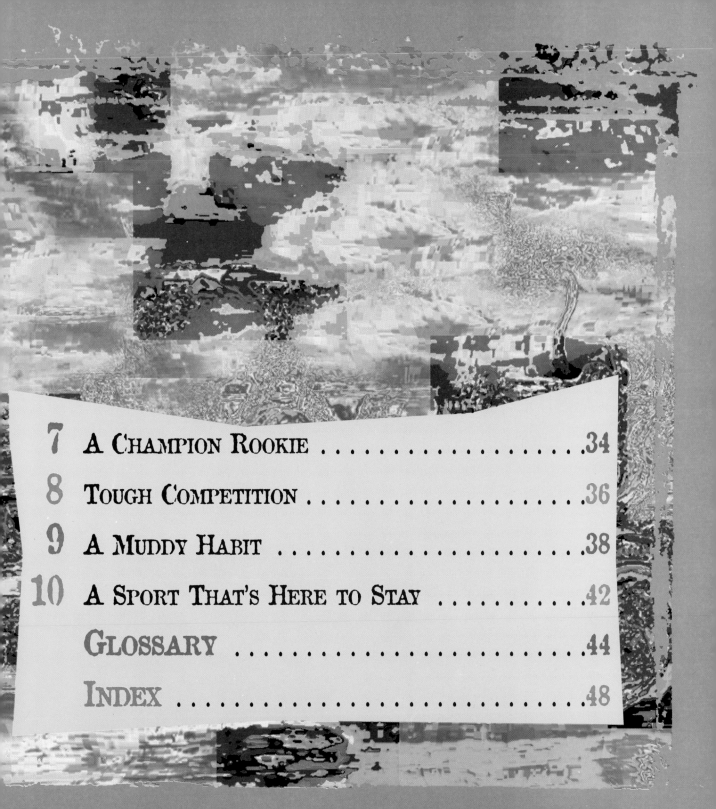

CHAPTER 1

IT'S NOT AS EASY AS IT LOOKS

Paul Shafer recognized the customer in his shop. It was the same man who came in almost every week looking for spare parts for his truck. The man's name was Tom Martin. He was a mud racer.

Paul operated an auto shop called Paul's Autoyard at the southern tip of Lake Michigan in Gary, Indiana. Paul bought **junker** cars and sold the parts to customers for a profit. While selling a few parts to Tom one time, Paul decided to strike up a conversation. The two men chatted about trucks and engines and discovered they had much in common. They even lived in the same town of Portage, about ten miles east of Paul's Autoyard.

Tom was competing on the mud-racing **circuit** operated by the United States Hot Rod Association (USHRA). He told Paul he was looking for a **sponsor**. A sponsor is someone who provides financial support in return for free advertising for his or her business. Paul thought about it for a minute, smiled at

Tom, and said, "I'll be your sponsor." Tom was thrilled. The 1988 season was starting, and Tom knew his truck, Mud Patrol, was powerful enough to win some events. Now he had a sponsor, too.

Tom didn't disappoint Paul. Mud Patrol roared to victory after victory, and Tom won the 1988 points championship. Then he won it again in 1989. Paul was pleased to be sponsoring a two-time champion. But he still didn't know much about mud racing.

Paul would often tell Tom that mud racing looked easy. He would say, "There's nothing to it. You drive through a mud puddle. Big deal." Tom tried to

convince his sponsor that mud racing was a lot tougher than it looked.

One day, Tom dared Paul to try mud racing himself. Paul accepted the challenge. They went to a fairground in Michigan for a local mud-racing competition. Forty trucks were entered. Tom let Paul drive Mud Patrol. Paul didn't know about mud racing, but he knew about other types of racing. He had been the Indiana stock car champion one year and the Illinois champion another year. How much different could mud racing be?

Paul took his place at the starting line. The green light flashed and Paul pressed down on the **accelerator** pedal. Mud Patrol hit the **mud bog** and lurched to one side. Paul jerked the steering wheel, which sent the truck careening the other way, and clear out of bounds. It all happened in a flash. Paul couldn't believe it. He had lost control of the truck.

"That truck has a lot more power than I thought," he said to Tom, who was nodding in agreement. "I've never driven something with so much **horsepower**."

Luckily for Paul, that first attempt was just a practice run. The real competition had yet to begin. And when it did, Paul was ready. He maintained control of Mud Patrol and powered his way to a third-place finish. Even Tom was impressed. He was quick to congratulate Paul and then joked, "Of course, if I had been driving, Mud Patrol would've finished first."

Paul had discovered a motorsport unlike any other. "After that experience," Paul says, "I knew right away that I was going to become a mud racer. It was too big a challenge to pass up."

11

Chapter 2

A Man Who Enjoys a Challenge

Rookie basketball players usually don't dominate the world of professional basketball. It takes golfers a few years to get used to the pressures of the pro tour. Even race car drivers need a while to learn the art of maneuvering through traffic against their shrewd veteran opponents. Not so with mud racers.

After Tom Martin won his third straight USHRA points title in 1990, his sponsor Paul Shafer bought Mud Patrol from him. Paul joined the mud-racing circuit the following season with Mud Patrol, while Tom raced another vehicle called Super Trooper. Tom's expertise carried him to his

fourth straight title, but Paul was right behind—finishing fourth overall and winning Rookie of the Year honors. Then in 1992, Paul beat Tom and everybody else with Mud Patrol to win the points title.

"My first race was at Madison Square Garden in New York, and I had never been in front of 10,000 people before," Paul says. "Everyone was on their feet, screaming and jumping up and down. I was really nervous that night. Now it seems like so long ago. Today I'm one of the best drivers

around—
maybe the best."

It seemed as if it happened overnight. Paul won 5 races during his rookie year; then he reeled off an amazing 11 victories in 1992. He held the points lead through the year and only once was in jeopardy of losing it. At a Sunday afternoon event in Omaha, Nebraska, late in the season, Mud Patrol crashed. The truck was moving at a blinding speed when the front tires lifted, air swept underneath, and Mud Patrol slammed into a wall. Paul was not hurt, but Mud Patrol was mangled. "I thought I had lost the points title right there," Paul says. With three events remaining, Paul still needed points to clinch the '92 title.

Paul loaded Mud Patrol into his trailer and drove all night to Indiana. He spent the next four days cutting the truck into pieces and welding it back together. Then he drove east and arrived in time for the two-day show at the Civic Arena in Pittsburgh, Pennsylvania. Paul wasn't sure how Mud Patrol would hold up. But he didn't baby it. He slammed into the mud pit at full speed and powered right through it. He took second place Friday night and third place Saturday night to clinch the yearly points title.

"I worked real hard, and I beat the best," Paul says of his triumphant 1992 season. "Until then I was just known as Tom Martin's sponsor. I

13

think the other drivers respected me after I won the title."

Paul's constant search for challenges brought him next to **monster trucks**. He built one in 1993, named it Monster Patrol, and joined the USHRA monster truck circuit. But he didn't stop mud racing. He competed in both sports! Monster truck and mud-racing events are often held at the same place. It makes for a long night of racing, but Paul is a tireless performer. He proved he had **endurance** by finishing third in the 1993 points standings in both sports!

He drove Mud Patrol and Monster Patrol again in 1994, along with monster truck Taurus. "In San Diego, I flipped Taurus and smashed it up,"

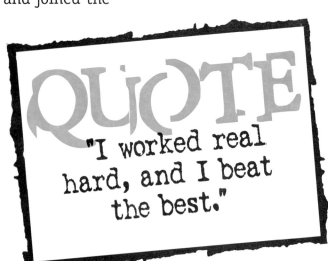

QUOTE

"I worked real hard, and I beat the best."

Paul says. But Paul went on to drive Mud Patrol to the mud-racing final match that night and pounded it through the pit to win the event. Then he drove Monster Patrol to the monster truck final match. "My body ached and I was so exhausted by then that I almost fell asleep at the starting line," Paul says. "I was too tired to even look for the green light. Predator beat me in the final."

So what does Paul prefer? Monster trucks or mud cars?

"That's easy," he says. "Mud cars don't get the credit they deserve. They're much harder to drive than monster trucks. I like mud racing much more."

DRIVERS MUST BE ALERT AT THE START-ING LINE, OR THEY'LL MISS THE GREEN LIGHT AND LOSE.

Chapter 3

How to Win the Race

Mud racing has evolved faster than any other motor-sport. Since its origin in the early 1980s, it has become popular with hundreds of thousands of racing fans. "Mud racing is getting to be as popular as monster trucks," says Julie Hoffmann, a spokeswoman for the USHRA. "People like to see the power of the engines combined with the flying mud."

Annual mud-racing events are held at huge stadiums such as the Astrodome in Houston, the Superdome in New Orleans, the Metrodome in Minneapolis, Jack Murphy Stadium in San Diego, Busch Stadium in St. Louis, and Anaheim Stadium in California. Sometimes mud racing is combined with monster truck racing or truck and tractor pulls for a major racing spectacle.

The object of mud racing today is not what it once was. In the sport's first few years, the goal was to see how far a vehicle could travel through the bog (or mud pit). The winner was the vehicle that traveled the greatest distance.

Today the winner is determined by the amount of time it takes to travel through the bog. Most bogs are 80 feet long, although a few are a little shorter or longer depending on the available space at an indoor arena. The bogs are usually 18 to 30 inches deep and 12 to 20 feet wide. Vehicles that fail to stay within the roped-off boundaries are **disqualified**.

Because almost all mud racers make it through the mud bog, a new rule was added a few years ago that requires the racers to stop within 80 feet after crossing the finish line. Vehicles that don't stop in time are disqualified. Mud racers can reach speeds in excess of 60 miles an hour. So stopping within the 80-foot boundary is as much of a challenge as racing through the bog.

GOLD FEVER DIGS FOR A PRECIOUS VICTORY.

17

An electronic timing system is used at all events. A set of lights similar to the **Christmas Tree** in drag racing is on a post at the starting line. But the lights do not signal the driver to start as they do in drag racing. The lights merely signal the driver that the course is clear. The timing system is activated when the vehicle crosses the starting line. It is deactivated when the vehicle crosses the finish line.

The order in which the vehicles race is determined by a drawing before the race. Drivers prefer to race early because the areas around the starting and finishing lines get slippery as the event progresses. The vehicles that record the four fastest times in the first round advance to the final round. These four drivers race once more to determine the winner. The winner usually completes the course in less than two seconds.

Sometimes the difference between winning and losing is one-thousandth of a second!

Points are awarded at each event to the vehicles according to where they finish. First place is worth 100 points; second place is 98 points; third is 97; fourth is 96; and so on. Racers who are disqualified for not staying within the boundaries or for going more than 80 feet beyond the finish line receive only 50 points. The vehicle that has the most points at the end of the racing season is declared the champion for that year.

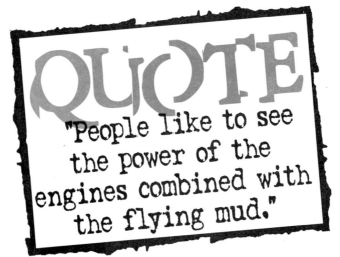

QUOTE

"People like to see the power of the engines combined with the flying mud."

DIRTY BIRD SOARS
TO THE FINISH LINE
WHERE THE
TIMING SYSTEM WILL
AUTOMATICALLY
RECORD ITS TIME.

THE KEY INGREDIENTS

The three key elements of mud racing are the driver, the vehicle, and the mud bog. Let's take a look first at the mud bog.

A *Sports Illustrated* magazine reporter was covering a mud-racing event at the Civic Arena in Pittsburgh one evening and offered the following recipe:

Mud-Bogging Track Mix
Ingredients: 122 truckloads of dirt
Directions: Spread the dirt evenly, 30 inches deep, in a pan the size of a hockey rink. Add 6,000 gallons of water. Stir.

The magazine writer was being humorous. But actually his recipe isn't far from the truth. It takes at least that much dirt and water to make a mud puddle big enough for a mud-racing competition.

Randy Spraggins, of Akron, Ohio, is the USHRA's expert track builder. Randy goes on a "dirt hunt" before the event to find the best dirt. Not all dirt is the same. Some is sandy, some has pebbles, some is moist, some is fine, and some is like clay. For a mud bog, Randy wants dirt that is sandy like topsoil. If he can't find this kind of dirt on the stadium grounds, he has to buy it.

After the dirt is hauled to the stadium, the bog is built using powerful equipment, such as loaders, bulldozers, rollers, grading tractors, backhoes, and excavators. Watching these mighty machines churn all that dirt can be as exciting as the race itself. Then the right amount of water is added. Not enough water and the bog will be too thick. Too much water and the bog will be too soupy. Randy has to be careful.

If you've ever been to a mud race, you arrived for the show long after the mud bog had been made. You probably had no idea that making a mud bog was such a big production.

ALL MUD BOGS ARE
NOT THE SAME. RACERS
LIKE SWAMP RAT MUST
BE ABLE TO HANDLE
THEM ALL.

The mud bog has not changed much since the sport began. That's not true for the vehicles. Shapes and styles have changed dramatically over the years.

The first mud racers were trucks sometimes as large as monster trucks. But drivers quickly realized that a lighter vehicle could move faster through the bog. Some drivers switched to Jeeps. Even they were too heavy, though. Today's mud racers look more like cars than

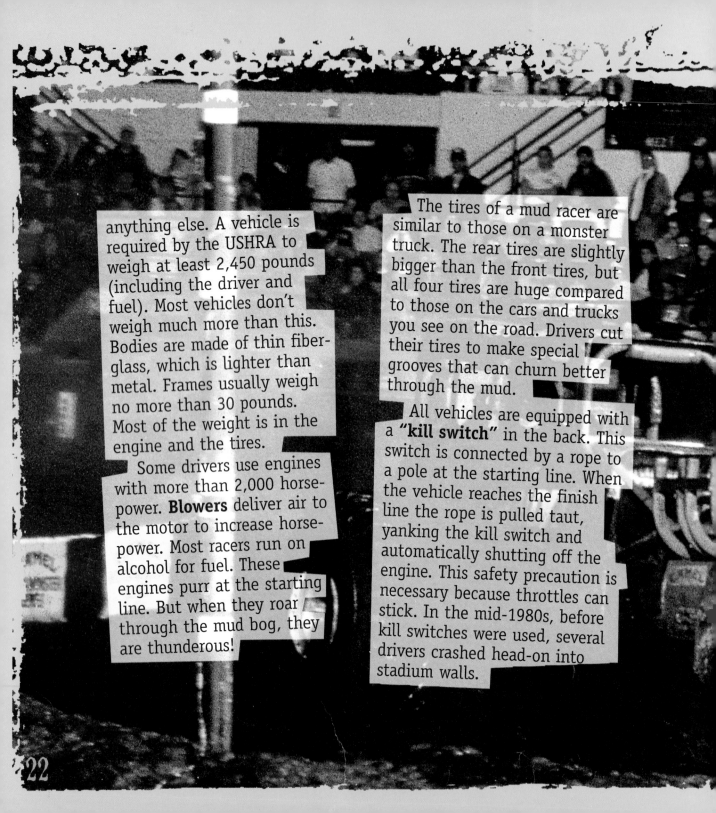

anything else. A vehicle is required by the USHRA to weigh at least 2,450 pounds (including the driver and fuel). Most vehicles don't weigh much more than this. Bodies are made of thin fiberglass, which is lighter than metal. Frames usually weigh no more than 30 pounds. Most of the weight is in the engine and the tires.

Some drivers use engines with more than 2,000 horsepower. **Blowers** deliver air to the motor to increase horsepower. Most racers run on alcohol for fuel. These engines purr at the starting line. But when they roar through the mud bog, they are thunderous!

The tires of a mud racer are similar to those on a monster truck. The rear tires are slightly bigger than the front tires, but all four tires are huge compared to those on the cars and trucks you see on the road. Drivers cut their tires to make special grooves that can churn better through the mud.

All vehicles are equipped with a **"kill switch"** in the back. This switch is connected by a rope to a pole at the starting line. When the vehicle reaches the finish line the rope is pulled taut, yanking the kill switch and automatically shutting off the engine. This safety precaution is necessary because throttles can stick. In the mid-1980s, before kill switches were used, several drivers crashed head-on into stadium walls.

MUD RACERS COME IN ALL SHAPES AND SIZES. BLUE RIBBON BANDIT IS A 1923 ALTERED CHEVY.

Chapter 5

Risky Business

A brutal accident in 1988 prompted the introduction of the kill switch. The site was the Kemper Arena in Kansas City, Missouri. The event was sponsored by USA Motorsports. The driver was Jeff Acker. The vehicle was Insanity.

Jeff had won several times with Insanity. He was an experienced driver. But all the experience in the world couldn't have prepared him for what was about to happen. Several drivers had already blasted through the bog when Jeff took his position at the starting line. He noticed that most of them had had trouble negotiating their mud racers through the pit. A few vehicles had even gone out of bounds.

All bogs are not the same. Depending on the type of dirt and amount of water used, some bogs are more slippery than others. Jeff knew by watching the other drivers that this bog was rough and lumpy. Still, Jeff knew how to drive only one way—hard. He cinched his **shoulder harness** and lap belt tightly and waited for the green light. When it flashed, Jeff jammed on the accelerator pedal and roared forward and into the bog. The bog was so rough that Insanity bucked hard like a wild bronco. Jeff's head snapped left and then right with such force that it knocked him out cold. Insanity made it through the bog successfully, but Jeff was unconscious and his right leg remained on the accelerator pedal. Insanity charged head-on into a concrete block.

Somehow Jeff was not seriously hurt. He had bumps and bruises but nothing more. His vehicle was another matter. Insanity was destroyed. "I put the truck in the hauling trailer in three pieces," Jeff remembers. "It was absolutely totaled!"

It took Jeff a month to get Insanity

MUD RACERS GO SO FAST
THAT ACCIDENTS ARE
BOUND TO HAPPEN.

back in shape and running again. The next event he entered was at the Madison County Coliseum in his home state of Wisconsin. Upon arriving he was instructed by race officials to connect a kill switch to the back of his vehicle. "They told me it was because of my crash in Kansas City that these kill switches were now required," Jeff says. "I couldn't believe I was the cause of it. I thought that was great."

The kill switch no doubt has saved countless drivers and vehicles from disaster over the years. "I never thought I would be part of mud-racing history, but I guess I am," Jeff says with a smile.

Jeff might be responsible for more than just the kill switch. It is partly because of his antics that mud racing is

25

WHEN DEVASTATION CROSSES THE FINISH LINE, A ROPE WILL YANK THE KILL SWITCH TO SHUT OFF ITS ENGINE.

29

such a popular motorsport. Jeff certainly wasn't the first to drive a truck through a mud puddle. But he may have been the first to do so in front of a track **promoter**.

As soon as Jeff got his driver's license at age 16, he bought a brand new 1979 black Chevy pickup and put big tires on it. Then he drove it to Great Lakes Dragaway in Union Grove, Wisconsin, for a race. It had been raining that day, and by the time Jeff arrived at the track, the race had been canceled. The dirt track was a muddy mess. Jeff was disappointed. He wanted so much to drive his new truck that he couldn't stand it. So he took it out on the track and drove right through the mud. Another truck driver who had come to race saw Jeff splashing through the mud. The other truck driver joined the fun. Then another driver brought his truck onto the track and then another. Pretty soon there were six trucks roaring up and down the muddy track. By now more than 100 people had gathered in the stands to watch. One of the spectators was "Broadway" Bob Metzler—the track promoter.

The people in the stands jumped up and down and cheered every time a truck splashed through a big mud puddle. And Broadway Bob began doing some thinking. "If people get this excited watching a truck splash through mud," Bob said to himself, "why not put on a show for them? Why not have trucks race through the mud?" Mud racing was born.

Within a month, Bob began hosting "mud drags" at Great Lakes Dragaway. Two trucks would line up side by side at the starting line and then race down a straightaway. It was just like drag racing. The only difference was the track. Instead of smooth asphalt—it was mud!

> ## QUOTE
> "I never thought I would be part of mud-racing history..."

FANS LOVE TO SEE ENGINES BURN AS THE RACERS POWER THROUGH THE PIT.

Chapter 6

The Father of Mud Racing

Jeff Acker became a top-notch mud racer. He finished third in the USHRA points standings in 1990 and then finished second in 1991. Today he races a 1923 altered body with a tube **chassis**. His vehicles have changed over the years, but their names are the same. Jeff says his vehicles will always be known as Insanity.

Jeff's toughest competition in the early years of USHRA competition was Tom Martin. While Jeff may have been one of mud racing's pioneers, Tom Martin will forever be known as the Father of Mud Racing. That's because Tom was the 1988 points champion—the first year the USHRA held a points series competition. Then to show it was no fluke, Tom won the yearly title again in 1989. He won it again in 1990. He won it for the fourth straight year in 1991. It wasn't until 1992 that the great champion was dethroned.

Tom built Mud Patrol and drove it to his first three titles before selling it to his sponsor, Paul Shafer. He then built Super Trooper and drove it to the '91 title. He continues to drive Super Trooper today along with another Mud Patrol vehicle.

"I drove or built the first five vehicle champions," Tom says proudly. "I have a lot of competitive blood in me, which drives me to be the best I can be."

Tom first began building racing vehicles at age

ten when he designed and built a go kart completely by himself. A few years later he was building dune buggies to race on the sandy shore of Lake Michigan, near his home of Portage, Indiana.

"I always wanted to drag-race," he says, "but they closed down the track by my house, and mud racing was the next available thing to do."

Tom joined the USHRA mud-racing circuit when it began. "I wanted to

TOM MARTIN BECAME THE FATHER OF MUD RACING WITH MIGHTY MUD PATROL.

get into mud racing while it was small and try to grow with it," he says.

Tom's first competition was on a cool Friday evening at Soldier Field in Illinois in 1985, where the Chicago Bears play football. Tom couldn't believe he was in the middle of the stadium driving a truck. He also was amazed at the number of people in the stands. A crowd of more than 40,000 had come to see these trucks splash through the mud. Tom was so nervous when his turn came to race that he almost snapped off the steering wheel. But he regrouped and then powered Mud Patrol through the bog in an impressive fashion. "When I saw and heard the thousands of people cheering, I knew this was the sport for me," he says.

QUOTE

"I have a lot of competitive blood in me ..."

Tom has been delighting crowds ever since. He has set records for most victories in a season, most points in a season, and fastest time through an 80-foot pit. "The more the people cheer, the more pumped up I get," he says.

Tom also has been an innovator. He was the first driver to sit at the rear of the vehicle to gain better traction. Now all drivers sit above the rear wheels. He also designed a tire tread pattern that expels the mud better than other tires. Now most competitors cut their tire tread in the pattern Tom created.

"Mud racing has been a great sport for me," Tom says. "I hope to compete against the best for a long time." Many would say Tom Martin is the best.

SUPER TROOPER RIPS THROUGH THE BOG ON ITS WAY TO ANOTHER VICTORY.

A CHAMPION ROOKIE

One of Tom Martin's mud-racing records—most wins by a rookie in a season—was broken in 1993. This came as no surprise to most of the drivers. After all, records are meant to be broken. But the racer who broke the record was a surprise to everyone. His name was Tony Farrell. The drivers all had the same question when the season began: "Tony *who*?"

Tony Farrell had never competed in a national mud race before. He was a true rookie when he showed up for his first race of 1993. But as we mentioned earlier, rookies on the mud-racing circuit have as much chance of winning as veterans. Tony proved that.

Tony had driven mud racers for a few years in his hometown of North Vernon, Indiana. And he was good at it. But the competition in North Vernon was not exactly the same as the competition in the Superdome or Madison Square Garden.

TONY FARRELL MADE A NAME FOR HIM-SELF WHEN HE WON A RECORD-BREAKING EIGHT RACES WITH BLUE RIBBON BANDIT.

Tony won eight times in his rookie season with a vehicle called Blue Ribbon Bandit. It was a 1923 altered Chevy with a 562-cubic-inch engine that produced 2,000 horsepower. In other words—it was powerful. "Before, I had one of the biggest, baddest trucks in the area," Tony said after the season. "Now I have one of the baddest trucks in the whole country."

Tony still drives Blue Ribbon Bandit today. He says the competition gets tougher every year. "Most of the cars I compete against are really steady," Tony says. "There are no good and bad weekends for them. They're good every weekend, so I have to be ready for them every time I go out."

One of the reasons for Tony's sudden success was his crew chief, Kevin Miller. Kevin had built hot rod cars with Tony 12 years earlier. Then they built a turbocharged engine that burns a special fuel called nitromethane for Blue Ribbon Bandit. Tony knew his vehicle was fast. He just didn't know how fast.

"This year has been a complete surprise to me," he said after receiving his 1993 championship trophy. "It was my first time competing indoors on a points series with a blower motor. I certainly never expected to walk away with the championship."

Neither did anyone else expect him to.

Chapter 8

Tough Competition

The first time that Matt Ward competed in a USHRA event, he crashed. His vehicle—Mystic Warrior—lurched sideways out of the mud pit and rolled over. "I was totally shocked," Matt says. "This was something that had never happened to me before."

It wasn't as if Matt had years of experience going into the race. His father, Preston Ward, had been racing Mystic Warrior in local events for eight years. "When Matt was 16, I told him anytime he wanted to drive, he should let me know," Preston says. "I wasn't feeling real well one night, so Matt drove." Matt was 17 at the time. A year later he joined the national circuit.

So how did the young rookie do? Well, as you know, rookies can be dangerous on the USHRA circuit. And sure enough, Matt Ward was another amazing rookie. He won more events—six— than any other driver and finished fourth overall in the points race. What else might you expect from someone in the engine-building business who hails from a town called Mechanicsburg in Pennsylvania?

The only reason Matt didn't finish higher than fourth was because he also led all drivers in disqualifications (which occur when a vehicle goes out of bounds or goes more than 80 feet beyond the finish line). Still, Matt's go-for-it style earned him the instant respect of his fellow mud racers.

"Matt has a super car and is doing a great job for a kid his age," four-time champion Tom Martin said during Matt's rookie year. "His lack of experience is the only thing keeping him from the top. He is a definite threat."

One of Matt's toughest defeats was in the final round at the Rosemont Horizon in Chicago in the last event of the season. Matt lost a heart-breaker to—who else?—another rookie! Alvin Esh beat Matt and the rest of the 15-car field to claim second place in the season's final point standings. "I had made up my mind going into this weekend that I was going to finish second," Alvin said after his victory. "Nothing was going to get in my way."

"Big Al," as he is known on the mud-racing circuit, didn't win six times like Matt Ward. But he also didn't get disqualified as many times. Alvin was the more consistent driver. That's why

he finished second overall and was named Rookie of the Year. He was also one of the few drivers who competed with a truck—a 1991 blue Chevy S-10 called Beef T Blue.

Alvin proved his rookie season was no fluke by running consistently in Beef T Blue to finish fourth overall in 1993. He came back strong again in 1994, and today is one of the most feared competitors in the country. "I'm as concerned about Beef T Blue as anybody," former champion Paul Shafer says. "No competitor is more fierce than Big Al."

BEEF T BLUE CARRIED DRIVER ALVIN ESH TO ROOKIE OF THE YEAR HONORS.

Chapter 9

A Muddy Habit

As we approach the twenty-first century, more drivers than ever before are joining the USHRA national circuit. The pride in building a championship mud racer, the thrill of powering through mud, the cheering of thousands of fans, and the friendships among the drivers are just too much of a temptation.

"It's a bad habit to get into," says racer Byron Tinkey. "It takes all of my free time and is very expensive. But I just can't give it up."

Byron started driving trucks through the mud in the early 1980s in his hometown of Coralville, Iowa. He joined the circuit several years later and experienced his biggest thrill in 1992 when he won all three races at the three-day event in Niagara Falls, New York. The name of Byron's vehicle?—Bad Habit.

There are plenty of talented mud racers today. Larry Jarrett from Perry, Oklahoma, might be the best mud racer on the circuit right now. His vehicle is a 1991 custom-built sprint car called Locomotion. Sometimes it seems more powerful than a train.

Jeremy Finley's nickname is "Wild Man," and he drives a souped-up 1932 Chevy coupe. "You never know what the racer will do," Jeremy says. "You can

LOCOMOTION—LARRY JARRET'S CUSTOM-BUILT SPRINT CAR—SOMETIMES SEEMS MORE POWERFUL THAN A TRAIN.

end up doing **wheelies** or head in any direction. It's scary every time you race. That's the thrill of it."

When Tom Meents isn't driving Mud Patrol for former champion Paul Shafer, he's driving his own vehicle—the popular red and white 1932 roadster known as Shake Me.

Bob Heisner competes in the odd-looking blue 1937 Fiat called Hot Tuna. Bob has already won the Championship Finals in Chicago with his 1,500-horsepower Chrysler engine, and Hot Tuna continues to show up in the final round at many events.

If the mud bog is rough, count on Tom Marsh to finish near the top with his 1923 Ford T pickup known as Intruder. "I like a track that is chewed up," Tom says. "It suits my racer better."

Melvin Brown is twice as likely to reach the final round as any other racer. That's because Melvin races two mud racers at each event. Melvin drives Red Heat, a red rear-engine dragster, and Blew Maxx, a blue Jeep. "It gets quite expensive if I crash or if I break something," Melvin says. It's also quite funny if Melvin faces off against himself in the final.

JEREMY FINLEY PLOWS THROUGH THE MUD IN HIS SOUPED-UP CHEVY COUPE.

MELVIN BROWN IS TWICE AS LIKELY TO WIN SINCE HE DRIVES TWO MUD RACERS: RED HEAT—AND THIS ONE, BLEW MAXX.

41

CHAPTER 10

A Sport That's Here to Stay

Mud racing is young compared to other motorsports, so it continues to experience many changes. For instance, sand has been used a few times recently in place of mud. The rules are the same—it just isn't as messy. Drivers are also more likely to pop wheelies in sand. One thing drivers definitely prefer about sand: They don't need to hose off their vehicles after the show.

"We held sand events at the Seattle Kingdome and in Florida and the reaction of fans was mixed," says USHRA spokeswoman Julie Hoffmann. "Some fans like to see the mud flying

SHAKE ME—THE RED AND WHITE 1932 ROAD-STER—IS A FAN FAVORITE.

around. Some like to see the wheelies in the sand."

Make no mistake. Sand or no sand, mud racing is here to stay. "It's real tough to top mud racing as a sport," says Todd Jarrett, a lifelong motorsports fan. "You've got engines, power, noise, mud—everything kids like. I mean, what kid doesn't like to play in the mud?"

And in case you thought mud racing was fake like pro wrestling, think again. Mud racing is real. Just ask Todd Marrion, the driver of Expect No Mercy.

"Usually if someone has never heard of mud racing, they just think it's a bunch of guys taking some ol' buggy out on a dirt field," Todd says. "When they actually see what it is, they're really impressed by the high technology, high-performance engines, and competitiveness of the sport. Mud racing is for real."

43

GLOSSARY

accelerator The foot pedal used to control the speed of a vehicle

blower The device that delivers air to the motor of a racing vehicle to increase horsepower

chassis The frame of a vehicle, which supports the body

Christmas Tree The system of lights at the starting line that signals when the race can begin

circuit The schedule of events in the mud-racing season

disqualified Eliminated by officials from competition, usually for breaking a rule

endurance The measured ability to sustain or keep going without fail

horsepower The way the power of an engine is measured

junker An old, dented, decrepit, or poorly running vehicle

kill switch The device that, when pulled by a cord, automatically shuts off the engine

monster truck A powerful truck that has giant tires and competes in the popular motorsport

mud bog The pit of mud that vehicles drive through in mud racing

promoter A person who organizes events for spectators

shoulder harness The strap of the seat belt that diagonally crosses the driver's chest

sponsor A person or company that provides financial support to a competitor

wheelie A maneuver in which the front end of a vehicle rises into the air

INDEX

4

AD	FF	MU
AV	GR	NC
BO	HI	SJ
CL	HO	CN L
DS AUG 0 4 '9?	LS	

THIS BOOK IS RENEWABLE BY PHONE OR IN PERSON IF THERE IS NO RESERVE
WAITING OR FINE DUE.

LCP #0390